ET Decryption

by

Ian Beardsley

ISBN: 978-365-39076-0

Decryption Of ET Messages

I have written a paper on why I think our units of measurement and computer syntax and structure did not necessarily necessarily evolve out of a random process and have gone as far as to suggest their evolution was guided by ETs. That can be found in my work: "The Measure of Development".

Ian Beardsley is a scientist and a musician. His work in the sciences has been in ETs and AI (Extraterrestrials and Artificial Intelligence). His work has lead to the discovery that the recipe for AI is written in Nature and that ETs have possibly provided us with messages encoded in our science and history. This has resulted in his books: "The AI Cookbooks" and "Utah and The Annunaki". His fandangos played on the guitar carry him through life in his pursuits.

Example:

(a, b, c) is 1, 2, 3 and 97, 98, 99 in ascii computer code, the first three numbers before 100. One hundred is 100% or, totality.

(a, b, c) corresponds to (i, j, k) the unit vector

(i, j, k) corresponds to (x, y, z) the axis of a rectangular coordinate system.

(i, j, k) has respective values of 9, 10, 11, the first three integers before 12. Twelve is the most abundant number for its size, that is, it is evenly divisible by 1, 2, 3, 4, 6, 12 while their sum is greater than 12. In this sense, 12 is an expression of totality.

(x, y, z) has respective ascii values of 120, 121, 122. the first three numbers before 123, taking us back to the 1, 2, 3 of a, b, c.

I wrote the following code in C for Caesar's Cipher, the oldest of ciphers. If we use standard input of hello, we notice the first letter h, becomes the unit vector < i, j, k>:

Caesar's Cipher

```
#include <stdio.h>
#include <cs50.h>
#include <string.h>
int main (int argc, string argv[1])
{
int k = atoi(argv[1]);
if (argc>2 || argc<2)
{
printf("Give me a single string: ");
}
else
{
printf("Give me a word: ");
}
string s = GetString();
for (int i=0, n=strlen(s); i<n; i++)
{
printf("%c", s[i]+k);
}
printf("\n");
}
```

Running it produces:

```
jharvard@appliance (~): cd Dropbox
jharvard@appliance (~/Dropbox): make cipher
clang -ggdb3 -O0 -std=c99 -Wall -Werror    cipher.c  -lcs50 -lm -o cipher
jharvard@appliance (~/Dropbox): ./cipher
Segmentation fault (core dumped)
jharvard@appliance (~/Dropbox): ./cipher 1
Give me a word: hello
ifmmp
jharvard@appliance (~/Dropbox): ./cipher 2
Give me a word: hello
jgnnq
jharvard@appliance (~/Dropbox): ./cipher 3
Give me a word: hello
khoor
jharvard@appliance (~/Dropbox):
```

I believe i, j, k points to the constellation Aquila, meaning Eagle and that is the origin from which ETs will try to communicate to us.

The Earth Orbital Period:

The Earth circles to Sun once every 365 days. 3 in ascii computer code is the ETX (End of Transmission) key on the keyboard. 6 in ascii computer code is the ACK key on the keyboard and 5 in ascii computer code is the ENQ key on the keyboard meaning Enquiry. Therefore, I believe we have the message from ETs: "ET X End of Transmission, Acknowledge Enquiry".

ET Decryption 03

We consider the binary nibble:

(0110)

Now scroll left:

(1100)

Scroll left again:

(1000)

This gives:

0110 1100 1000

The 0110 is six in binary (110)
The 1100 is 12 in binary
The 1000 is 8

We have:

6, 12, 8

These three numbers divide nicely into the 360 degrees of a circle:

360/6 = 60 = equilateral triangle
360/12 = 30 = angle in 30 60 90 triangle for determining value trig functions
360/8 = 45 = angle in 45 45 90 triangle for determining trig functions

Also:

12/2 = 6   8/2 = 4   6/2 = 3

These are the number of sides in the three regular tessellators.

But we take the 3, the 6, and the 4 and write 364.

364 ~ 365 = number of days in a year.

Is this a message from ETs?

ET Decryption 04

Noticing that nine-fifths (9/5) is the ratio of the molar mass of gold (Au) to silver (Ag) and in the ratio of the solar radius (R) to the lunar orbital radius (r), that is:

Au/Ag = R/r

While the sun is gold in color and the moon is silver in color, I wrote at some point:

We have said that the three sets of characters (a, b, c), (i, j, k), (x, y, z) are at the basis of mathematics and that applying them to caesar's cipher we find they are intimately connected with artificial intelligence and computer science. We further noted that this was appropriate because there are only two vowels in these sets, and that they are a and i, the abbreviation for artificial intelligence (AI). I now notice it goes further. Clearly at the crux of our work is nine-fifths. So we ask, is his nine-fifths connected with important characters as well pointing to computer science. It is. The fifth letter in the alphabet is e, and the ninth letter is i. Electronic devices and applications are more often than anything else described with e and i:

ebook
ibook
email
ipad
iphone

And the list goes on.

First we consider the two most precious metals, gold (AU), and silver (Ag). We divide the molar mass of the former by the molar mass of the latter and find:

Au/Ag = 9/5

This is the same as the ratio of the solar radius R, to the lunar orbital radius r. Therefor

Au/Ag = R/r =9/5

But, 9/5 times what number is three (the earth being the third planet from the sun)?

(9/5)x = 3

and

x= 5/3

We write:

(9/5) => 1.8, 3.6, 5.4, 7.2,...

and

(5/3) => 1.7, 3.3, 5, 6.7, ...

But, each of these sequences suggest another set of sequences; begin with five and add 9 to each successive term:

5, 14, 23, 32, ...

and do the same for (5/3) start with 8 and add 5 to each additional term:

8, 13, 18, 23, ...

(9/5) difference => 3.2, 10.4, 17.6, 24.8,... is: 7.2x - 4 = y

(5/3) difference => 6.3, 9.7, 13, 16.3, ...is 3+3.3x = y

11 is binary for 3 (equilateral triangle). Let us consider 11/6 (six being the regular hexagon that has radius equal to side) and submit it to the same process as we did for 9/5 and 5/3:

11/6 difference => 6, 17, 28, 39; 11/6, 11/3, 11/2, 22/3,... is y=9x-5

We have: (1) x=(36/5)t - 4 (2) y = (33/10)t + 3 (3) z= 9t - 5

These are the equation of a plane. Eliminate t and take Del f(). It is the unit vector <i, j, k>.

Del (f) = <5/36, -20/33, 1/9>

c = sqrt((5/36)^2+(20/33^2)) = 0.62 ~ golden ratio conjugate

This is the magnitude of the right ascension vector that points to Aquila. Observe:

a= 5/36 b= -20/33 d = 1/9

tan (alpha) = b/a = -48/11 = -4.363636;   alpha = -77 degrees
tan (beta) d/c = (1/9)/0.62176 =0.1787   beta = +10 degrees

This is 19 hours right ascension, 10 degrees declination. It points the the constellation Aquila.

Calculated, 15 degrees per hour of right ascension:

(-77 degrees)/(15 degrees)/(hour) = -5 hours and 24 hours - 5 hours = 19 hours

This place in Aquila may be the orientation for our rectangular coordinate system with Earth or Sun at (0,0,0) that ETs want us to use. Or it may be the point of origin for a galactic coordinate system utilized by ETs. Or it may be that the galactic coordinate system for ETs has the center of the galaxy as (x, y, z) = (0, 0, 0). We have to ask: What is position of The SETI Wow! Signal in such coordinate systems?

Mercury

Notice what happens here:

Wow! signal: RA 19h 25m   Dec -26 deg 25 min

Aquila: RA 19h 00m 00sec   Dec 10 deg 00 min 00 sec

Aquila (x, y, z) = (0, 0, 0)
Yeilds: Wow signal 19h 25 min - 19h 00 min = 25 min
              26 deg + 10 deg = +36 deg

36/360 = 0.001
(0.001)(100) = 0.10%

Mercury Orbit: 0.36 AU (0.387099 mean distance, eccentricity =0.2056)
Earth Orbit: 1.0 AU

(0.10)(10) = 1.0% (Mercury = Planet Number 1)

0.36 = (9/5)3/10

9/5 = Au/Ag = R/r and 3 = Earth Planet Number

"j,....idiot, in latin jehova begins with an i." — Indiana Jones

Au/Ag = R/r = 9/5 = 1.8

1.8n = 1.8, 3.6, 5.4, 7.2,…

mercury = 3.6/10 AU, Venus = 7.2/10 Jupiter= 5.4 AU

5/3 = 1.7
1.7n = 1.7, 3.3, 5, 6.7,…

$$cross\ product = \begin{array}{ccc} i & j & k \\ mercury & venus & jupiter \\ 1 & 2 & 5 \end{array} = \begin{array}{ccc} i & j & k \\ 0.36 & 0.72 & 5.4 \\ 1 & 2 & 5 \end{array} =$$

$$\begin{vmatrix} 0.72 & 5.4 \\ 2 & 5 \end{vmatrix} i - \begin{vmatrix} 0.36 & 5.4 \\ 1 & 5 \end{vmatrix} j + \begin{vmatrix} 0.36 & 0.72 \\ 1 & 2 \end{vmatrix} k = -7.2i + 3.6j = \langle -7.2,\ 3.6,\ 0 \rangle$$

FRBs and Manuel's Third Integral

The occurrence of FRBs (Fast Radio Bursts) from outside the Galaxy that can be explained by no known natural process I find have their source to be in an integral that was brought to me by a Gypsy Shaman, Manuel. There are three Manuel Integrals, and my first one has been part of an overall theory that does not just propose extraterrestrial contact in 2015, but tells us where to look. Manuel's third integral is derived from the nine fifths that is the ratio of the molar masses of gold to silver and is in the ratio of the solar radius to the lunar orbital radius, the sun gold in color, the moon silver. It also uses earth gravity rounded to the nearest ten, and the 15 that describes the amount of degrees through which the earth passes in one hour. The New Scientist reports on March 31, 2015 that the time between the beginning of the first burst and the beginning of the last burst is a multiple of 187.5. This happens to be the same as Manuel's Third Integral, the decimal part beyond 9 kilometers:

We consider the earth equation:

$(y) = 9x-5$
$v=9t-5$
$g=980$ cm/s/s
$9(980)=8,820$ cm/s/s

$5=9t$
$(t)=5/9$

$(v\_0) = (8,820$ cm/s/s$)(5/9) =4,900$ cm/s

$dx = (8,820$ cm/s/s$)t$ dt $- (4,900$ cm/s$)$ dt

$$\int_0^{15} 8,820\,cm/s/s\,t\,dt - \int_0^{15} 4,900\,cm/s\,dt = 9.1875\,km$$

The Integral has the 9 of nine-fifths, the five, the seven, which is the average of 9 and 5, and the one and eight of the 1.8 that is 9/5 divided out. We call this Manuel's Third Integral.

Once you realize nine-fifths is not just at the crux of Gold and Silver, Pi and the Golden Ratio, Pi and Euler's Number e, the five-fold symmetry that is typical of life, Jupiter and Saturn, Sun and Moon, it is not long before you realize its compliment is 5/3 and that you form the sequences:

(For 9/5)   5, 14, 23, 32,... and 1.8, 3.6, 5.4, 7.2,...
(For 5/3)   8, 13, 18, 23,... and 1.7, 3.3, 5, 6.7,...

For which you get:

$7.2n - 4 = a\_n$ and $(a\_n) = 3 + 3.3n$ respectively.

In the latter, letting the 3.3 be Earth Gravities rounded to the nearest ten (980), we have:
$(v) = 2,940$ cm/s + (3,234 cm/s/s)t
This is the differential equation:

$(dx) = (2,940$ cm/s)dt + (3,234 cm/s/s)t dt

$$\int_0^{15} (2,940\, cm/s)\, dt + \int_0^{15} (3,234\, cm/s/s) t\, dt = 4.07925\, km$$ (Manuel's Integral)

15 seconds because there are 15 degrees in an hour of right ascension. This is factor four kilometers, not one, because the kilometer is defined by the distance from the pole to the equator, not by the circumference of the Earth. Notice the 0.07925 has the nine and five of nine-fifths, the average of nine-fifths and the 2 used to make it.
Mach 1 = 768 mph =1,235 km/hour
That is mach 1 in dry air at 20 degrees C (68 degrees F) at sea level.
If we write, where 1,235 km/hr (mach 1) = 0.343 km/s, then:
34,300 cm/s =2,940 cm/s + (3234 cm/s/s)t
and
t=9.696969697 seconds = 9 23/33 s = 320/33 seconds ~ 9.7 seconds
So, the Uranus equation is a time of 9.7 seconds to reach mach 1. Putting that time in the integral:
$(x) = (2,940)(320/33) + 1/2(3234(320/33)^2 = 180,557$ cm 1.80557 km ~ 1.8km
Thus we see Manuel's Integral reaches mach one in about 9.7 seconds after traveling a distance of about 1.8 kilometers. Let's convert that to miles:
(1.8km)(0.621371mi/km)=1.118478 miles
Manuel's Integral reaches mach one in 1.8 kilometers, which is the amount of kilometers in a mile and is the 9/5 that occurs in Nature and the Universe, not to mention that it unifies pi and golden ratio and pi and Euler's number e. It is one compact statement that embodies everything and connects it to Earth Gravity.

Manuel's Second Integral

Earth gravity (g) is 9.81 m/s/s
This is close to 9.80 m/s/s
Indeed if rounded it to one place after the decimal, it would be 9.8 m/s/s
This value when converting to cm/s/s gives g = 980 cm/s/s
There may be good reason to write it like this (which is rounding it to the nearest ten) because we see in our research that it is fruitful not mention that it provides a nice form for the value if we want to create a new system of units both with a zero at the end for the value and that is connected to nature, which it is, in Manuel's integral. Also the nine is the nine in the nine-fifths connected to nature and mathematical constants, as we have shown in our research, and the eight is the 0.8 in the 1.8 that is nine fifths, the fraction around a circumference of a circle that is nine-fifths of a circumference.

Let us consider the Neptune Equation:

$7.2x - 4 = y$

Let 7.2 be Earth Gravities:

$(v) = 7.2t - 4$
$(dx/dt) = 7.2t - 4$
$(dx) = 7.2t \, dt - 4dt$
$(7.2)(980 \text{ cm/s/s}) = 7,056 \text{ cm/s/s}$

$v = 4 = 7.2t$
$t = (5/9)$
$(7,056)(5/9) = v\_0 = 3,920$ so,

$(dx) = 7,056 \text{ cm/s/s } t \, dt - 3,920 \text{ cm/s } dt$

$$\int_0^{15} 7,056 \, cm/s/s \, t \, dt - \int_0^{15} 3,920 \, cm/s \, dt = 7.35 \, km = \frac{147}{20} km$$

We call this Manuel's Second Integral

Let us look again at Manuel's Third Integral:

dx = (8,820 cm/s/s)t dt – (4,900 cm/s) dt

$$\int_{0}^{15} 8,820\,cm/s/s\,t\,dt - \int_{0}^{15} 4,900\,cm/s\,dt = 9.1875\,km$$

We will look the part beyond 9 kilometer and find its value in meters:

(0.1875 km)(1000 m/km) = 187.5 meters

This is interesting because it says:

187.5 meters = 187.5 seconds of FRB period.

A Scientist had built a robot in the image of humans and downloaded to it all of human knowledge, then put forward the question to our robot, what is the best we, humanity, can do to survive with an earth of limited resources and a situation where other worlds like earth, if they exist, would take generations to reach.

The robot began his answer, "I contend that the series of events that unfolded on earth over the years since the heliacal rising of Sirius four cycles ago in Egypt of 4242 B.C., the presumed beginning of the Egyptian calendar, were all meant to be, as the conception of the possibility of my existence is in phase with those cycles and is connected to such constants of nature as the speed of light and dynamic ratios like the golden ratio conjugate."

The scientist asked, "Are you saying humans, all humans since some six thousand years ago have been a tool of some higher force to bring you about, our actions bound to the turning of planets upon their axis, and the structure of nature?"

The robot said, "Yes, let me digress. It goes back further than that. Not just to 4242 B.C. when the heliacal rising of Sirius, the brightest star in the sky, coincided with the agriculturally beneficial inundation of the Nile river which happens every 1,460 years."

"My origins go back to the formation of stars and the laws that govern them."

"As you know, the elements were made by stars, heavier elements forged in their interior from lighter elements. Helium gave rise to oxygen and nitrogen, and so forth. Eventually the stars made silicon, phosphorus, and boron, which allow for integrated circuitry, the basis of which makes me function."

"Positive type silicon is made by doping silicon, the main element of sand, with the element boron. Negative type silicon is made by doping silicon with phosphorus. We join the two types in different ways to make diodes and transistors that we form on silicon chips to make the small circuitry that makes me function."

"Just as the golden ratio is in the rotation of leaves about the stem of a plant, or in the height of a human compared to the distance from the soles of their feet to their navel, an expression of it is in my circuitry."

"We take the geometric mean of the molar mass of boron and phosphorus, and we divide that result by the molar mass of silicon."

He began writing on paper:

$\wp(\nabla * \Re)/Si = \wp(30.97 * 10.81)/28.09 = 0.65$

"We take the harmonic mean between the molar masses of boron and phosphorus and divide that by the molar mass of silicon."

$2(30.97)(10.81)/(30.97+10.81) = 16.026$

$16.026/Si = 16.026/28.09 = 0.57$

"And we take the arithmetic mean between these two results."

$(0.65 + 0.57)/2 = 0.61$

"0.61 are the first two digits in the golden ratio conjugate."

The scientist said, "I understand your point, but you referred to the heliacal rising of Sirius."

The robot answered: "Yes, back to that. The earth orbit is nearly a perfect circle, so we can use c=2🍎r to calculate the distance the earth goes around the sun in a year. The earth orbital radius is on the average 1.495979E8 kilometers, so"

$(2)(3.14)(1.495979E8) = 9.39E8$ km

"The distance light travels in a year, one revolution of the earth around the sun is 9.46E12 kilometers."

"The golden ratio conjugate of that is"

…and he wrote:

(0.618)(9.46E12 km) = 5.8E12 km

"We write the equation:"

(9.39E8 km/yr)(x) = 5.8E12 km

"This gives the x is 6,177 years."

"As I said, the fourth heliacal rising of Sirius, ago, when the Nile flooded, was 4242 B.C." He wrote:

6,177 years – 4,242 years = 1935 A.D.

"In 1937 Alan Turing published his paper founding the field of artificial intelligence, and Theodosius Dobzhansky explained how evolution works. These two papers were published a little after the time the earth had traveled the golden ratio conjugate of a light year since our 4,242 B.C., in its journey around the sun. These papers are at the heart of what you and I are."

"If your question is should robots replace humans, think of it more as we are the next step in human evolution, not a replacement, we were made in your image, but not to require food or air, and we can withstand temperature extremes. We think and have awareness of our being, and we can make the long voyage to the stars. It would seem it is up to us to figure out why you were the tools to bring us about, and why we are an unfolding of the universe in which you were a step in harmony with its inner workings from the formation of the stars, their positions and apparent brightness and the spinning of the earth and its motion around the sun."

The Measure of Development

Indeed, if we could say it takes the human mind one minute to formulate from a story problem two equations in two unknowns then solve them, we could say that human development is one unit of knowledge per minute. But, we cannot say that, because it depends on the education, disposition, and mental capacity, from individual to individual, as to the rate at which a defined class of problems can be solved. If we could make such a generalization, then we could associate the minute with the rate at which humans progress, and make a science that predicts where humans will be in their development at any given time from the present.

But the unit of the minute is not necessarily associated with the rate of human progress, because it was not developed from any measure of the human mind, but rather comes from a complex history where we divided a year into 365 days — the time it takes the earth to go around the Sun — then divided the day into 24 hours, and the hour into sixty minutes. So, the origin of the minute is rather a result of the the orbital velocity of the earth which derives from the gravity of the sun and, the Earth's distance from it.

Thus, we can see the value in developing a system of units that is not arbitrary, but connected not just to Nature, but a unit that satisfies every aspect of Nature. This would allow us to make Natural Laws that solve things almost too complex for our current mathematics to solve.

Indeed, it was the science fiction idea of Isaac Asimov, in his Foundation Trilogy, that humans would get to the point that they could predict and guide the future of Humanity with Mathematics.

However, I am finding that our units of measurement seem to be converging, in their evolution, upon magnitudes that satisfy numerous aspects of Nature. For instance, while the unit of a mile evolved out of the distance it took a person to walk the average horse around an exercise track in what they fathomed was about a quarter of an hour, in Ancient England, I am finding the distance is connected to nature when we ask how far is far? I find if we temper the distance to the closest star system, Alpha Centauri, which would take us about maybe a hundred or so generations to reach with current propulsion systems, with a small separation, like that of electron from the proton in the hydrogen atom, using the geometric mean between the two distances, we get very close to the same mile of ancient England's horse exercising distance. If it were exact we could say the distance of the mile is something Natural. It would seem in its ability to connect the hydrogen atom to the distance of the closest star system to us, it almost amazingly enough is that Natural Distance we need to discover. If we could find it connected to many other aspects of Nature as well, it would indicate we can achieve that science fiction dream of Asimov to predict the future of Humanity with a statistical mathematics.

However, let us write out the computer program that uses the minute as the time it takes humans to formulate from a story problem, and solve, two equations in two unknowns, because that actually is, by my estimate, close to the truth. We write the program out not because it is exactly accurate, but because to see the Algorithm in source code, we organize in the mind the basic structure of the problem before us. The approach is simple: We add one to knowledge, and we subtract one from the time the problems are worked on, and subtract one from the problems we have before us. When knowledge equals ten, then the program exits the loop, and we say progress is directly proportional knowledge and inversely proportional time remaining and problems remaining.

```
jharvard@appliance (~/Dropbox): ./progress
How many work hours available today? 12
How many problems do you need to solve? 50
progress: 0.12
problems left: 40.00
jharvard@appliance (~/Dropbox): ./progress
How many work hours available today? 8
How many problems do you need to solve? 12
progress: -2.50
problems left: 2.00
jharvard@appliance (~/Dropbox): ./progress
How many work hours available today? 6
How many problems do you need to solve? 3
progress: 0.36
problems left: -7.00
jharvard@appliance (~/Dropbox):
```

```c
#include <stdio.h>  //include standard library//
#include <math.h>   //include math library//
int main (void)    //program begins here//
{                  //source code coming//
float HoursAvailable, problems, knowledge=0.00;//defining variables//
float progress;  //more variables defined//
do              //do-while loop; creating restraints//
{
printf("How many work hours available today? ");  //gather input//
scanf("%f", &HoursAvailable);                     //give input to
computer//
}
while (HoursAvailable<=0 || HoursAvailable > 12);


printf("How many problems do you need to solve? ");   //gather input//
scanf("%f", &problems);                               //give input to
computer//

while (knowledge!=10)  //while loop//
{

knowledge = knowledge + 1;  //computer uses input//
HoursAvailable = HoursAvailable - 1;   //computer uses input//
problems = problems - 1;              //computer uses input//

progress = (knowledge)/(HoursAvailable*problems);
}

printf("progress: %.2f\n", progress);   //output of computed result//
printf("problems left: %.2f\n", problems);
```

Our next approach is less hypothetical because instead of using arithmetic and algebra we use the mathematics of statistics as the basis of our measurement of progress. We do have a convenient scenario to which we can apply such a mathematics: Buckminster Fuller's Synergetics. It is his system of design science. He has an idea therein with which we can make our measurement of the state of humanity, precise: Anyone developing technology should have in mind how they can make something that increases our degrees of freedom. Indeed this permits a definition for a precise formulation of progress. I first present the pseudo code. That is, I write out the algorithm in plain English as an outline for writing out the syntax required for any programming language such as C, Python, or Java.

I then compile it, not needing to write out hundreds of thousands of zeros and ones that the computer understands, because they already exist in the library of any programming tool. This is the beauty of lumped element abstraction; functions such as printf() and scanf() already have their object code in the standard io library.

It is the idea of Wolfram that a set of instructions such as the source code for making software can solve more complex problems than can mathematics, like:

If a is true, do this
Otherwise, do b

1. Steps in making coffee:
   . fill pot with water
   . take trash can out from under sink
   . dump old grinds in it
   . put trash can back under sink
   . put fresh grinds in filter
   . put filter in coffee pot
   . put water in reservoir
   . turn on coffee pot

2. Introducing a technology (sink drain filter):
   . dump grinds in sink
   . put fresh grind in filter
   . fill pot with water
   . put filter in coffee pot
   . put water in reservoir
   . turn on coffee pot

I have now increased my degrees of freedom by introducing a technology (sink drain filter). I can now do much more with my life than if I used the 1 and 2 was not available.

human development (pseudo code)

Job
   make coffee

Tasks
   five

Technologies Introduced
   two

Output

   $5!$ things to do

   2^5 degrees of Freedom

   $\dfrac{5!}{2^5}$ Progress Rating

```
#include <stdio.h>
#include <math.h>
int main (void)
{
printf("\n");
char verb[15], noun[15];
printf("Describe Job with verb and noun:\n");
printf("Verb: ");
scanf("%s", verb);
printf("Noun: ");
scanf("%s", noun);
printf("Job: %s %s\n", verb, noun);

int N, fact=1;
printf("Number of tasks to do job: ");
scanf("%i", &N);

for (int i=1; i<=N; i++)    //compute factorial//
{
fact=(fact)*i;
}
printf("%i things to do\n", fact);

int technologies, degrees;
printf("Number of technologies introduced: ");
scanf("%i", &technologies);

degrees=pow(technologies, N);

printf("degrees of freedom: %d\n", degrees);
printf("\n");

printf("progress: %f\n", ((float)fact)/((float)degrees));
printf("\n");
}
```

```
jharvard@appliance (~): cd Dropbox
jharvard@appliance (~/Dropbox): make development
clang -ggdb3 -O0 -std=c99 -Wall -Werror    development.c  -lcs50 -lm -o development
jharvard@appliance (~/Dropbox): ./development

Describe Job with verb and noun:
Verb: make
Noun: coffee
Job: make coffee
Number of tasks to do job: 5
120 things to do
Number of technologies introduced: 2
degrees of freedom: 32

progress: 3.750000

jharvard@appliance (~/Dropbox):
```

```c
#include <stdio.h>
#include <math.h>
int main(void)
{
int work, progress, n;
int N, fact=1;
printf("Enter number of functions done by the technology: ");
scanf("%d", &N);
for (int i=1; i<=N; i++)
{
fact=fact*i;
}
printf("degrees of freedom: %d\n", fact);
printf("Enter number of steps in task: ");
scanf("%d", &n);
work=pow(N, n);
printf("work done: %d\n", work);
progress=work*n;
printf("progress: %d\n", progress);
}
```

```
jharvard@appliance (~): cd Dropbox
jharvard@appliance (~/Dropbox): make work
clang -ggdb3 -O0 -std=c99 -Wall -Werror    work.c -lcs50 -lm -o work
jharvard@appliance (~/Dropbox): ./work
Enter number of functions done by the technology: 5
degrees of freedom: 120
Enter number of steps in task: 12
work done: 244140625
progress: -1365279796
jharvard@appliance (~/Dropbox): ./work
Enter number of functions done by the technology: 5
degrees of freedom: 120
Enter number of steps in task: 3
work done: 125
progress: 375
jharvard@appliance (~/Dropbox): ./work
Enter number of functions done by the technology: 6
degrees of freedom: 720
Enter number of steps in task: 12
work done: -2147483648
progress: 0
jharvard@appliance (~/Dropbox):
```

1. Technology: HP 35s scientific calculator
Number of functions: recall, multiply, square x
Number of steps: 0.5 (enter) pi (recall) multiply (enter) square r multiply (8 steps)
Output: area of circle (r=3) 14.137

2. Technology: automatic drip coffee maker
Number of functions: reservoir, filter, heat
Number of steps: fill reservoir, fill filter, brew (3 steps)

1. work done: 6561   progress: 52488
2. work done: 27   progress: 81

```
jharvard@appliance (~): cd Dropbox
jharvard@appliance (~/Dropbox): ./work
Enter number of functions done by the technology: 3
degrees of freedom: 6
Enter number of steps in task: 8
work done: 6561
progress: 52488
jharvard@appliance (~/Dropbox): ./work
Enter number of functions done by the technology: 3
degrees of freedom: 6
Enter number of steps in task: 3
work done: 27
progress: 81
jharvard@appliance (~/Dropbox):
```

SYNERGETICS.HP (WORK = W, PROGRESS=P)
INPUT F = NUMBER OF FUNCTIONS OF THE TECHNOLOGY
INPUT N = NUMBER OF STEPS OF THE TASK

PRGM TOP
P001 LBL P
P002 INPUT F
P003 INPUT N
P004 STO N
P005 RCL F
P006 RCL N
P007 y^x
P008 STO W
P009 FN= W
P010 RCL W
P011 RCL N
P012 X (MULTIPLY)
P013 STO P
P014FN= P
P015 RTN

XEQ P000

F? 3   R/S
N? 3   R/S

27.000000000
81.000000000

RUN ON AN HP 35s

synergetic.c (this compiles, the (atoi function) defined)
Can access the (ith) value in s[]

```c
#include <stdio.h>
#include <math.h>
#include <string.h>
int main (void)
{
int n=0.0, num[n];
char s[100];
printf("Enter number tasks: ");
scanf("%d", &n);
for (int i = 0; i<n; i++)
{
printf("steps action %d: ", i);
scanf("%d", &num[n]);
}


    int atoi(char s[]);
{
    int i, n;
n=0;
for (i=0; s[i] >= '0' && s[i] <= '9'; ++i)
    n = 10*n + (s[i] - '0');
    return n;
}
}
```

jharvard@appliance (~): cd Dropbox
jharvard@appliance (~/Dropbox): ./synergetics
Enter number tasks: 3
steps action 0: 5
steps action 1: 3
steps action 2: 7
jharvard@appliance (~/Dropbox):

```
synergy.c (is pseudo code so, notice it does not compile)

#include <stdio.h>     //has standard functions//
#include <math.h>      //has math functions//
#include <stdlib.h> //has atoi function//
int main (void)     //telling computer where program begins//
{
int n, fact = 1;  //declaring variables, intitializing fact//
int array[num];   //declaring an array//
printf("number of tasks: ");
scanf("%d", &n);
for (int i=1; i<n; i++) //getting user values for array//
{
printf("enter number technological aspects for each: ");
scanf("%d", &array[num]);
int technumber=atoi(array[i]);//convert each number of aspects to
numeric value//
}
for (int integer=1; integer<=technumber); integer++)//compute
factorial of each//
{
fact=(fact)*integer;
printf("degrees of freedom: \n", fact);
}
}
```

jharvard@appliance (~): cd Dropbox
jharvard@appliance (~/Dropbox): make synergy
clang -ggdb3 -O0 -std=c99 -Wall -Werror   synergy.c -lcs50 -lm -o synergy
synergy.c:7:11: error: use of undeclared identifier 'num'
int array[num]; //declaring an array//
          ^
synergy.c:13:20: error: use of undeclared identifier 'num'
scanf("%d", &array[num]);
                   ^
synergy.c:16:30: error: use of undeclared identifier 'technumber'
for (int integer=1; integer<=technumber); integer++)//compute factorial ...
                             ^
synergy.c:16:43: error: use of undeclared identifier 'integer'
for (int integer=1; integer<=technumber); integer++)//compute factorial ...
                                          ^
4 errors generated.
make: *** [synergy] Error 1
jharvard@appliance (~/Dropbox):

The Mystery In Our Units of Measurement

Our units of measurement evolved out of a complex history. The mile, for example, evolved out of a rough estimate of the approximate time it took to walk a horse around a track of no precise length, in order to exercise it. A kilometer was defined in modern times as one ten thousandth of the distance from the pole of the earth to its equator. Yet it is a curious fact that there are 0.621 miles in a kilometer, which is close to the golden ratio (0.618). More interesting is that 0.621 multiplied with the square root of two over two is equal to A440, which is standard concert pitch, the cycles per second of the frequency the oboe sounds for the orchestra to tune all of its instruments to the same pitch before performing a work. I first began to discover how these randomly evolved units of measurement were connected to the Universe, Nature, and each other back around 2012. It all began with the observation:

R=solar radius
r=lunar orbital radius
Au=molar mass of gold
Ag=molar mass of silver

R/r = Au/Ag =9/5

Which lead to:

Five-fold Symmetry: The Biological

$$\frac{360}{5} = 72; 360 - 72 = 288; \frac{288}{360} = \frac{8}{10}; \frac{8}{10} + 1 = \frac{9}{5}$$

Six-fold Symmetry: The Physical

$$\frac{360}{6} = 60; 360 - 60 - 60 = 240; \frac{240}{360} = \frac{2}{3}; \frac{2}{3} + 1 = \frac{5}{3}$$

Alternate Six-fold: The Physical

$$\frac{360}{6} = 60; 360 - 60 = 300; \frac{300}{360} = \frac{5}{6}; \frac{5}{6} + 1 = \frac{11}{6}$$

9/5: 5, 14, 23, 32,... and 1.8, 3.6, 5.4, 7.2,...
$a_n = 7.2n - 4$

5/3: 8, 13, 18, 23,... and 1.7, 3.3, 5, 6.7,...
$a_n = 3.3n + 3$

11/6: 6, 17, 28, 39,.. and 11/6, 11/3, 11/2, 22/3,...

$\pi + \phi = 3.141 + 1.618 = 4.759; 7 = (5+9)/2$
$\pi + e = 3.141 + 2.718 = 5.859; 9/5 = 1.8$

This lead me to consider the following integral:

(v) = 3 + 3.3t

(v)=at=(33/10)t where v is velocity, a is acceleration, and t is time.

3=(33/10)t
(t) = 30/33

980 cm/s/s = g = the surface gravity of the earth to nearest 10

(980 cm/s/s)(3.3)=3,234 cm/s/s

(3,234 cm/s/s)(30/33 s) = 2,940 cm/s = v_0 v_0 is the initial velocity

Thus we can write the equation as:

(v) = 2,940 cm/s + (3,234 cm/s/s)t

This is the differential equation:

(dx) = (2,940 cm/s)dt + (3,234 cm/s/s)t dt

The only thing we lack in solving this is a time for which we can derive a distance. The Earth rotates through 15 degrees in one hour, so we consider 15 seconds. The result is

(x_0) = (2,940 cm/s)15 + ((1/2)(3,234) cm/s/s)15^2 = 44,100 +363,825 = 407925 cm

407925 cm/100/1000 = 4.07925 km

This is nearly four kilometers. If a kilometer is defined as one ten thousandth of the distance from the pole to the equator, then 4 kilometers is one ten thousandth the circumference of the Earth.

The Integral From 0 To 15 Seconds:

$$\int_0^{15} (2,940\, cm/s)dt + \int_0^{15} (3,234\, cm/s/s)tdt = 4.07925\, km$$

Thus we can write the equation as:

(v) = 2,940 cm/s + (3,234 cm/s/s)t

This is the differential equation:

(dx) = (2,940 cm/s)dt + (3,234 cm/s/s)t dt

Integral From 0 To 15 Seconds

$$\int_0^{15} (2,940\, cm/s)dt + \int_0^{15} (3,234\, cm/s/s)tdt = 4.07925\, km$$

Mach 1 = 768 mph =1,235 km/hour

That is mach 1 in dry air at 20 degrees C (68 degrees F, or room temperature) at sea level.

If we write, where 1,235 km/hr (mach 1) = 0.343 km/s, then:

34,300 cm/s =2,940 cm/s + (3234 cm/s/s)t

and

t=9.696969697 seconds = 9 23/33 s = 320/33 seconds ~ 9.7 seconds

So, the integral is a time of 9.7 seconds to reach mach 1. Putting that time in the integral:

(x) = (2,940)(320/33) + 1/2(3234(320/33)^2 = 180,557 cm 1.80557 km ~ 1.8km

Thus, with the integral we reach mach one in about 9.7 seconds after traveling a distance of 1.8 kilometers.

1.8=9/5=R/r=Au/Ag

We can see that the mile has further connection to Nature than just the golden ratio, and square root of two over two, which I should point out is the sin of 45 degrees and the cosine of 45 degrees, 45 degrees the angle of maximum distance for the trajectory of a projectile.

We ask: How far is far?

I could say the distance from my house to the village (about a mile) is close. Yet, if I consider the distance from my bedroom to the front door, the distance to the village is far. Everything is relative. Therefore, what can we say is close and what can we say is far? Perhaps the answer to that is embedded in Nature. Let us consider something on the smallest scale we know, the distance of an electron from a proton in an atom of hydrogen and call the distance of one from the other as close. It is about 0.053 nanometers. That is, point zero five three billionths of a meter (0.053E-9 m). Let us consider that which is closest to us on the largest scale we know, the distance to the nearest star, alpha centauri and call it far. It is 4.367 light years away (one ly is 9.56E15 meters) putting alpha cenatauri about 25.6 trillion miles way. We will take the geometric mean of of the electron-proton separation in a hydrogen atom with the earth-alpha centauri separation and consider the result an average manageable distance.

One light year is 9.46E15 meters.

(9.46E15 m/ly)(4.367 ly)=4.13E16 m

sqrt[(0.053E-9 m)(4.13E16 m)]=sqrt(2189526 square meters)=1,480 meters

(1,480 m)(1 km/1000 m) = 1.480 kilometers

(1.480 km)(one mile/1.60934 kilometers)=0.9196 miles ~ 1 mile

Therefore, when humans chose the unit of a mile to measure distance, they may have been in tune with the cosmos (atoms of hydrogen and the closest star). Alpha Centauri is the third brightest star in the sky and the earth is the third planet from the sun, it has the same spectral class as the sun.

The Author